Country House Cats

Other books by Richard Surman available from Collins

Cathedral Cats
Church Cats
Cloister Cats
Dog Collar
Secret Churches

Country House Cats

Richard Surman

Collins

Collins

a division of HarperCollins Publishers

77–85 Fulham Palace Road, London w6 8jb

www.collins.co.uk

First published in Great Britain in 2008 by
HarperCollins Publishers

1

A catalogue record for this book is available from the British Library.

isbn-13 978-0-00-725917-5

Design by Susie Bell

Printed and bound in Hong Kong by Printing Express

Collins

Contents

Introduction

It was with some apprehension that I approached the idea of *Country House Cats*. Surely the historic houses and stately homes that grace the British countryside would be decidedly more in favour of horses and dogs – animals associated with traditional country pursuits – than cats? 'Lord and Lady Langford keep dogs, and currently there are four Dalmatians and a Jack Russell living here so, as you might imagine, cats are an endangered species here,' was the polite but emphatic response to an early approach at Bodrhyddan Hall in North Wales; from Hatfield House in Hertfordshire, 'Your book sounds very interesting, but, unfortunately, we are very much a doggy household!'; from Lancashire's Leighton Hall, 'If you ever start on dogs, please get in touch again as we have numerous dogs

and many doggy stories we could tell you.' Cats, if any, would be in short supply, I feared!

However, all was not lost; tales emerged that suggested that many a noble home, mansion and manor had capitulated in the face of feline persistence. Some were cat havens from the start like Feeringbury Manor in Essex, home of Sybil, a Lady Bracknell sort of cat. At Tissington Hall in Derbyshire, Sir Richard

FitzHerbert allows three cats to drift around his feet almost unnoticed, while, in the Cotswolds, Sir Cyril and Lady Kleinwort almost moved their Siamese cats into Sezincote before themselves.

Other country houses have cats in the way that they might have ancient retainers or staff: cats that are there to work. In general, the country house cat lives in a practical no-nonsense environment. Alcibiades at Kentwell Hall is under no illusion that his flushing out of rodents is his raison d'être at the Hall. There is the extraordinary too: Saddam, the Erddig cat, is deaf and blind, but still happily wanders the grounds with Glyn Smith, the head gardener, using vibration and scent as alternative senses. Jock lives at Chartwell as a result of a request that there should always be a 'Jock' there in memory of Sir Winston Churchill. All the cats and places featured here have their own unique characteristics, from the grand and imposing, to the modest and unassuming, and even to the downright eccentric.

I'd like to thank everyone who helped me in the course of preparing *Country House Cats*. A big vote of thanks to Ian Metcalfe and Ruth Roff at HarperCollins, for their continued enthusiastic support (despite a sneaking suspicion on my part that neither are particularly mad about cats); thanks, too, for all the kindness and hospitality shown to me by everyone I visited. I'd especially like to express my gratitude to

English Heritage and the National Trust for Scotland for their enthusiastic cooperation, and my long-suffering family for their support and interest too.

For Blanca

Emily
Arley Hall

'No amount of time can erase the memory of a good cat, and no amount of masking tape can ever totally remove his fur from your couch.'

Leo Dworken

I had always imagined that the notion of a cat in one of Britain's country houses or stately homes was a bit of an anomaly. Arley Hall, the family home of the Warburtons, was ever thus – a place for dogs – much to the frustration of Jane Foster, the sister of Lord Michael Ashbrook, current owner of Arley Hall. Jane's youthful affection for cats was partially fulfilled by Heidi, a Persian tortoiseshell. But Heidi kept on having kittens, and was eventually banished; as compensation, Jane was given a collie called Fran, whom she remembers as, 'very affectionate but pretty stupid'. Fran never got the hang of house-training so she, too, didn't stay very long.

Jane's first opportunity to have a cat – Lucy – came when she was living in London's Notting Hill Gate,

HISTORY

The original Arley hall was built in the 15th century by Piers Warburton, and has been in the same family ever since. It was substantially rebuilt in the 19th century by Rowland Egerton-Warburton and, unusually for the period, embodies features such as patterned brickwork, ornate chimney stacks and heraldic carvings reminiscent of Tudor architecture. Napoleon III spent a winter at Arley, and the Emperor's bedroom can be seen in the upper part of the house. One unusual feature of the house is the chapel, which was designed by the noted Victorian architect Anthony Salvin, a leading light of the return to authentic Gothic styles of architecture, and restorer of (among other places) the Tower of London. Mention must be made of the gardens too – some eight acres of formal garden and a further six or seven acres of woodland garden.

with her husband Charles. Lucy came from an Exeter cat rescue centre (the family had a cottage in Devon) and enchanted the whole family, so much so that Jane and Charles Foster's eldest daughter Antonia named *her first daughter* after the cat! This caused a whole lot of confusion, with daughter Lucy turning up for cat feeding, and cat Lucy turning up to be got ready for school; from thereon it was established that, whatever cat might come in the future, no one in the family would have the same name as the cat. Lucy gave everyone a few heart-stopping moments: the Foster's London home was a tall, terraced Victorian villa, and, as a kitten, Lucy scaled the heights to visit Antonia, whose bedroom was about 80 feet (almost 25 metres) above street level; being a curious kitten, the first thing Lucy did was to fall out of the window, landing – incredibly – without any injury whatsoever. Lucy's most important role, however, was to provide the children with an excuse not to do anything around the house. 'I can't come now; Lucy's sitting on my lap!'

After Lucy's demise, Jane started to look for a replacement. So Emily came, looking just like Lucy, but with no human namesake in the house. She is a most unusual-looking cat. Emily has two halves, the front being mostly white and the rear being mostly black, as if she had been painted by someone with an unsteady hand, who was constantly changing their mind about which half should be black and which should be white, and who eventually lost patience.

Emily spent a short while living with Jane in London, before the family moved to Arley Hall.

Arley Hall is at the centre of a sizeable estate, surrounded by landscaped parkland and outstanding gardens, the different parts of which reflect the varied horticultural and aesthetic interests of individual family members. Emily, far from being overawed by this move from central London to the wide open spaces of the Cheshire plains, switched seamlessly from being a city cat to a true country house cat. The large marmalade cat that habituated the gardens sought at first to woo (unsuccessfully) and then to subjugate the sassy young city feline, who taught him a thing or two about close combat, until Emily finally took the estate for her own.

Emily likes a good walk, and can often been seen strolling through one of the many different garden areas: the sculpturesque holly walk; scrambling around the Rootree, a 19th-century garden laid out to resemble a miniature mountain landscape; and particularly the Herb and Scented gardens, where she sits almost intoxicated by the exotic range of smells that waft through the air. She is a gregarious cat too. Though normally put out when there is an event in the house, Emily blithely trots around to the other side of the house, and finds a way of joining in: she features in countless wedding photographs, and likes to think that her presence at business conferences adds to the gravitas of corporate planning strategy. Visitors, too, get the full treatment from Emily, who sits on the counter of the gift shop, handing out advice on souvenirs. She has even had a special bed made for her by one admirer – a champagne crate lined with hand-crocheted material.

Arley Hall is also a much sought-after venue for filming and product launches. Several automotive companies have launched new models there, and one of these launches provided Emily with her greatest opportunity for public appearance to date. The scene was set in the courtyard outside the main entrance to the Hall: lights, music, a shrouded vehicle, and champagne for the visiting motor industry press, most of whom could have told the excited marketing executives from the car company that the outline of the soon-to-be-revealed new car was a bit, well, bulbous. But the moment came and, to the usual pizazz, the shroud was whisked away, revealing a new car, complete with a blinking Emily, who had been happily snoozing on the bonnet. Ah, Emily, you really do know how to steal the show.

Rooney
Bateman's

"'I meant," said Ipslore bitterly, "what is there in this world that truly makes living worthwhile?" Death thought about it. "Cats," he said eventually, "Cats are nice.'"

Terry Pratchett, **Sourcery**

When Elaine Francis was appointed Assistant Property Manager at Sissinghurst Castle Garden, it was the first time that she had settled in a place that was not a flat, and she seized the opportunity to fulfil a long-held ambition – to have a cat. She found Jasper housed by himself – because of his unusually large size – at a nearby animal rescue centre. Not only was he large and no longer in the bloom of youth, but he also had a large lump; he was a lucky cat to have found such a kind-hearted benefactress. He adored living at Sissinghurst: he hobnobbed with garden visitors, and dallied along the children's garden trails, even being immortalised on one of the worksheets handed out to visiting school groups. One of his favourite spots in the garden was on the doorstep of Harold Nicolson's

HISTORY

Bateman's was built in the 17th century, probably by a Wealden ironmaster (iron ore was found in abundance underneath the local clay, and the medieval Sussex ironmasters were prolific makers and suppliers of cannon, nails and horseshoes). The interior is rich with oak panelling, reflecting the local abundance of the oak tree, which was known as the 'Sussex weed'. Having left America after an acrimonious family row, Rudyard Kipling acquired the house for himself and his American wife, Carrie. Bateman's represented seclusion and privacy for the Kiplings, a place where Rudyard Kipling could write, and where the couple might come to terms with the death of their six-year-old daughter. Kipling lavished much attention and money on the gardens, creating a working watermill, and assembling a notable collection of motor cars.

garden cottage, where he would sunbathe, nose gently twitching as the heady scents of garden plants drifted by. Jasper eventually died at Sissinghurst, and Elaine found another rescue cat – five-year-old Rooney.

Rooney is a broadband tabby, with a girth of white separating his rear from his front. He was the bereaved 'baby' of an old lady, and ended up in the animal shelter, with no sure prospect of adoption thanks to his age. In came Elaine, and Rooney's prospects immediately looked up. After three weeks at Sissinghurst, he moved with Elaine to their new home, Rudyard Kipling's celebrated Bateman's. Their first

accommodation was an old cottage at the bottom of the garden, and Elaine's fears that Rooney would fail to settle after a second move proved groundless. A few days later Rooney was pleading to be let out. Elaine decided to let things run their course, and off Rooney went. He didn't go far: the wild garden was a fabulous playground for Rooney, who, in the course of his explorations, also discovered the working watermill, where he spent hours watching flour being milled. Elaine and her partner Al were, however, puzzled by Rooney's odd habit of completely disappearing each Sunday, until a little bit of detective work revealed that he simply went next door to have Sunday lunch with the head gardener! It was only a matter of time before he took himself up to the house, where he made immediate friends with the office staff, and where he now has a second bed – a sort of kitty igloo and food stop. If the weather is bad Rooney simply sits at the office door, gloomily waiting until someone hears his desperate wailing.

From the office, Rooney discovered the footpath leading visitors to the house and gardens: as soon as the house opens, he takes up a strategic position, stretched out full length across the path, giving a homely welcome and revelling in the inevitable, ensuing attention. Elaine has more conversations with visitors about Rooney than about the house. One of Rooney's office friends, Fiona, is a regular outside companion: he often walks with her to and from the ticket office and down to the mill. And Rooney is not the only cat. One of the gardeners, Andy, has two called Jeeves and Wooster, but they tend to keep their own company away from the house.

As is the case with many country houses, there are 'events'. Bateman's is no exception, and Rooney is not the only cat in this book to display thespian tendencies: on two occasions – once during *A Midsummer Night's Dream*, and the other during a production of *The Railway Children* – Elaine spotted Rooney heading determinedly for the stage. Prompt action, involving a crouching dash and interception frustrated Rooney's attempts to join the cast, and now, when there is theatre in the garden, there is also a companion production – Rooney kept indoors.

Seeing Rooney stroll along the many garden paths, one is tempted to think of Kipling's famous story 'The Cat that Walked by Himself', but Rooney is the very antithesis of this selfish, aloof and rather one-dimensional animal portrayed by Kipling, whose understanding of, and contact with, cats was limited by his passion for terriers. But still, it is a pleasant notion to have an animal in the house of a writer whose early work characterised a broad palette of animals so vividly, most notably in the *Just So Stories*.

Chester and Bertie
Brodsworth Hall

'Cats are the ultimate narcissists. You can tell this by all the time they spend on personal grooming. Dogs aren't like this. A dog's idea of personal grooming is to roll in a dead fish.'

James Gorman

Chester is the cheery cat who lives with Michael Constantine, his wife Alison and their two daughters Emily and Evie. He's glossy black, with a wonderful white bib and bootees: a cat, one might say, who dresses for dinner. He came from the RSPCA to Brodsworth – a house with a long and sympathetic tradition of domestic animals. The Thellusson family was clearly fond of their pets: there's a little pets' cemetery in the gardens, with inscribed tombstones. Chester, however, took a while to accustom himself to his grand and extensive surroundings at Brodsworth. He initially had trouble with heights, both those he chose to scale, and those that he was chased up. Twice Chester has had to be rescued from trees, once in the dark from an enormous storm-tossed pine tree. He's

HISTORY

Brodsworth Hall is a grand Victorian country house, which replaced an earlier 18th-century house. It was built in the Italianate style at the behest of Charles Thellusson, and it followed the vogue of emulating Queen Victoria's new summer home Osborne House on the Isle of Wight. The Hall, situated not far from Doncaster, in former coal-mining country, has been the subject of extensive and sympathetic restoration, and refreshing touches of family life abound. Reassuring signs of wear coexist comfortably with the fruits of restoration – English Heritage does a magnificent job here. The drawing room, the dining room and the south hall were all clearly designed to impress, while the library – a favourite of the last owner, Sylvia Grant-Dalton – is cosy and homely.

fallen off the stable-block roof, having climbed up there on a ladder, and regularly performed inadvertent ski jumps off other roofs. It took him a while to appreciate that having claws is no great advantage on a steep, sloping slate-tiled roof.

Around the house, on terra firma, Chester has plenty to occupy himself. He isn't allowed to go round the house, although he always tries; he conceals himself in a dark part of the main hall, waiting to tack himself quietly on to a house tour, but the eagle-eyed guides always spot him, diverting him kindly but firmly to the office, where a notice proclaiming 'Chester in Residence' is then hung on the door. Chester doesn't

care; he likes going into the office because the site supervisor Pam always has a cup of cold coffee ready for him. And, after slurping his coffee, he's quite content to be ushered outside. Actually, outside is where most of the action takes place: in the gardens he walks around with visitors (although if they go too near the stables, Chester waits for them a little way off); then there are the events. Sunday band concerts, classic car rallies, the illuminated gardens in the autumn evenings – Chester enjoys them all. The car rallies are an opportunity to snooze on the warm bonnet of a Bentley or a Rolls-Royce, a habit not all car owners appreciate, especially when Chester leaves a trail of muddy paw prints on these lovingly hand-polished vehicles. As for his garden walks, it could be Chester's earlier experiences of tumbling off the stable roof that causes him to display some reluctance to go near the stables, but the more likely reason is Bertie.

Bertie, a black, tan and white hotchpotch *female* cat with a misleadingly gentle gaze, lives with the head gardener Dan Booth and partner Leanne in a stable-yard apartment. Bertie had been seen on frequent occasions around the stables, and it was thought that she was a village cat, but, as time went by, she got thinner and thinner, and Dan decided to take her in. Bertie was ready for residence, wolfed down her food, hopped up on laps and … that was it. At this time Chester was still mooching around the stables, and Bertie didn't like it at all. The two cats had a couple of pretty foul-mouthed stand-offs, after which Bertie found an open upstairs window through which she could clamber on to the rooftops; unlike Chester, Bertie quickly learnt to negotiate the slippery tiles, and the two cats now content themselves with swearing and glaring at one another: Bertie on high and Chester down below.

Bertie has other things on her mind than Chester at the moment. Not long ago, Dan returned to his apartment and Bertie's miaows of greeting turned to open-mouthed horror as a very enthusiastic Labrador puppy followed Dan through the door. Millie the puppy was delighted to see Bertie, and, despite having been cuffed around the nose several times, simply couldn't appreciate that Bertie doesn't want to play. Not even with the toys that Millie brings her. They all squeak at unexpected moments, and Bertie's nerves are a bit frazzled by all this unwanted attention. So Bertie sits up high, ignoring Millie, while Millie stands wagging underneath, doggedly squeaking every toy she can find to attract Bertie's attention; she then goes and eats Bertie's food, which is really adding insult to injury. As for Bertie and Chester, the gardens are large enough for both cats to wander without too much risk of bumping into each other, and, if Bertie finds Millie too much, she wanders down to the ticket office to spend the night with the security staff.

OPENING PAGE AND LEFT
Chester enjoying the grounds
ABOVE
Bertie near the stables

Missy, a.k.a. Newton
Cairness House

'Prose books are the show dogs I breed and sell to support my cat.'

Robert Graves

When painter and art historian Julio Soriano and historian and journalist Khalil Hafiz Khairallah acquired Cairness House, in the sweeping coastal countryside of Buchan, they knew that they were taking on a massive restoration project. A grand neoclassical house, Cairness had been neglected for decades, to the extent that the Scottish Civic Trust classified the house as a Building at Risk in 1991. What work had been done on the house in previous years was designed mainly to cover up more fundamental structural problems. Water ingress, dry rot and damp reigned supreme, especially in some of the upper parts of the house, which were close to collapse. Julio and Khalil moved into the house as soon as they had purchased it as a test of whether or not it was feasible

HISTORY
Built between 1791 and 1797 to designs by architect James Playfair, Cairness replaced an earlier house of 1781 by Robert Burn, which was largely incorporated into the new scheme. The park was laid out by Thomas White, a follower of Lancelot 'Capability' Brown and the building shows a strong influence of the French architects Étienne-Louis Boullée and Claude Nicholas Ledoux. Cairness House was commissioned by Charles Gordon of Cairness and Buthlaw and was part of a 9,000-acre estate that included the village of St. Comb's and the Loch of Strathbeg, today an important nature reserve. The Gordon family sold the estate in 1937 to the Countess of Southesk. After the Second World War, the house gradually fell into serious decline. A major long-term restoration programme of the house and grounds was instigated by new owners in 2001.

to restore. It was an eerie place. Not only did Cairness have an esoteric and mystical past, but it had been colonised by birds, insects and rodents; these could be heard at night scuttling along the damp upper galleries and staircases, behind wall panelling and above the remaining intact ceilings, their claws and squeaks intensifying the already mysterious atmosphere. During the day they were almost as bold, invading the kitchen and other downstairs rooms, using a network of secret passages and spaces behind walls. The solution was two kittens from Drummuir Castle Farm. As Julio is an artist, they decided to name the kittens Winsor and Newton.

The two kittens were delighted to find that, already in residence, was a soulful border collie called Ardkinglas. Border collies are not particularly tolerant of cats, being more used to the feral variety that inhabit farm buildings, but the pleasure shown by these two lively kittens on first seeing Ardkinglas was completely disarming: he resigned himself to becoming a cat cushion. Sadly, Winsor died at a young age, and Julio decided that Newton without the Winsor didn't make much sense, so Newton became Missy. And Missy, now a full-grown cat, still regards Ardkinglas as a living mattress, taking long naps stretched out full length on this obliging dog's back.

Of course, the point of having the cats at Cairness was the increasingly audacious nature of the marauding rodents. Things had got so bad that, whenever a dish was set out to cool on the kitchen table, there would be a mouse party. Winsor and Newton invited themselves too, much to the dismay and surprise of the carousing mice; gradually the mice were driven back to haunt the derelict parts of the house. And, as works started on the roof – replacing and repairing the 51 cast-iron chimney cans shaped liked Doric columns – and restoring more and more rooms to their former glory, so Missy has gained the upper hand.

Missy has all the space she needs, frequently roaming the house and gardens in company with Ardkinglas. For a cat, Cairness is a glorious place: while there's the considerable comfort of the restored areas, mostly in the main block, there is also a fortresslike semicircular service wing at the back, in whose courtyard stands an ice house in the style of the Athenian Temple of the Winds. Missy is busy patrolling this area now, engaged in a constant crusade to keep the ever-optimistic tide of mice at bay. The restored parts of the house, thoughtfully and beautifully furnished, are now open for guided tours, and the visitor is quite likely to come across someone sitting reading a newspaper, with Missy curled up beside them, and Ardkinglas fast asleep on the carpet. There is no need to contrive a 'lived-in' look at Cairness, because it really is a home.

Marmalade
Capesthorne Hall

'Animals are such agreeable friends – they ask no questions, they pass no criticisms.'
George Eliot

Stephen Caldwell is a no-nonsense sort of chap. As one of the gardeners at Capesthorne Hall in Cheshire, he had always declared that he would never have pets; now he has Marmalade, a striped ginger-and-white cat who arrived at Capesthorne as a stray. Even Stephen can't recall what persuaded him to adopt Marmalade, although I wonder whether it might have something to do with Marmalade's large, Cleopatra-like green eyes.

Whatever the reason, Marmalade is here to stay. And what is more, she sticks to Stephen like glue; wherever Stephen goes, there goes Marmalade too. She's not even put off if Stephen is driving a tractor, and, although she doesn't go as far as sitting on the tractor with Stephen, Marmalade contentedly trots alongside

HISTORY

Capesthorne Hall, a striking Jacobean-styled house dating from the earlier part of the 18th century, is the family home of the Bromley Davenports, whose ancestors have lived on the site since medieval times. The original design was by the Smiths of Warwick. In the 19th century it was altered by Edward Blore, an architect and antiquarian whose other works included Buckingham Palace and Lambeth Palace. In 1861 a major fire destroyed all but two wings of the hall and Anthony Salvin rebuilt the main part of the hall as it appears today. Capesthorne houses an eclectic and interesting collection of paintings, furnishings, tapestries and sculptures, principally of Rococo, Regency and Jacobean origin.

as Stephen and the tractor career around the estate. The hall administrator Gwyneth Jones says that it's never been easier to locate Stephen: one just looks out for the splash of orange, or listens for Marmalade's constant chatter with Stephen, who always says he hasn't a clue what she's saying!

Capesthorne Hall is the ancestral home of William Bromley Davenport, Lord Lieutenant of Cheshire, and

his American-born artist wife Elizabeth, and is set in one hundred acres of parkland, in which there are gardens, lakes and a charming Georgian chapel. And, during the season, numerous events are held at Capesthorne, ranging from weddings and classic car rallies to outdoor performances of Shakespeare and craft fairs. To all of these Marmalade is drawn like iron to a magnet. Within a few weeks of her arrival Marmalade had acquired an unexpected champion. She had wandered nonchalantly into the courtyard of the Hall during a reception; someone tried to shoo Marmalade out, but Elizabeth Bromley Davenport, who paints under her maiden name EB Watts, sprang to his defence. It was a kind and welcoming act, but perhaps not surprising from an artist whose paintings, much reproduced as cards and prints, bear such titles as *Cats with Pasta and Rocket*, and *Hen in Salad Nest*. It was, if you like, an official endorsement of Marmalade's resident status.

Marmalade is not entirely without guile and, for a modestly built cat, shows remarkable audacity. One of her recreational activities is dog baiting: there is nothing that Marmalade likes better than to sit impassively out of range of a tethered dog, encouraging it to reach ever shriller levels of hysteria. Dogs have been known to lose their voices and collapse in exhaustion after trying in vain to break free of their leads in order to chew out (or on) an unruffled Marmalade. She takes this further too: adjacent to the estate is a five-acre caravan park, where visiting

caravaners are permitted to bring their dogs. There are strict rules about where dogs can be exercised: adjoining parkland is permitted; the estate grounds and gardens are not. This means that, when in the caravan park, all dogs have to be kept from wandering. Nine times out of ten this means keeping them on a fixed leash – even at feeding time; even when the food bowl is slightly out of reach; even when Marmalade decides to finish the dog food for them (which she does very slowly, rolling her eyes in pleasure as she savours yet another mouthful). It is said that there have been some astonishingly rowdy nights at the Capesthorne Hall caravan park.

Marmalade has a classic feline attribute – insatiable curiosity. She tries to join in weddings, is always peering over the shoulders of anglers on the estate ponds, is a regular at the craft fairs (where she'll usually manage to find someone selling soft furnishings), and frequently visits the estate home farm, where she has rather noisy assignations with a large black cat. So maybe one day soon there'll be a whole tribe of little Marmalades creating mayhem with the caravaners' dogs.

Jock IV
Chartwell

'I like pigs. Dogs look up to us. Cats look down on us. Pigs treat us as equals.'
Winston Churchill

Churchill was a man who liked an odd assortment of animals – parrots, budgerigars, and, most of all, cats. His first cat at Chartwell was called variously 'Mr Cat', 'the marmalade cat' or 'Tango'. Visitors to the house can see him depicted sitting at the table with Sir Winston and his wife Clementine in William Nicholson's painting *Breakfast at Chartwell*. Rumour has it that Churchill used to try out his speeches on 'Mr Cat'. While working on his memoirs, he could be seen with a budgerigar on his head, a ginger cat asleep on his lap, and a poodle stretched out at his feet. As well as the marmalade cat of Chartwell there was Clementine's Siamese cat Gabriel; Churchill described the relationship between his and his wife's cat as a state of 'armed neutrality'. However, it was a gift from

HISTORY

Chartwell's fame lies entirely in the fact that it was the much-loved country residence of Winston Churchill and his wife Clementine, who bought it in 1924, principally for the glorious views from the south and east of the house over the Weald of Kent. The Churchills modernised it, particularly by the addition of a garden wing, which created a set of wonderfully light and airy rooms, gently and calmly furnished by Lady Churchill. In the 1930s Churchill converted one of the estate buildings into a studio, which is also open to visitors. The main house is a Victorian mansion – some think it rather gloomy – and its interest lies mainly in the contents: a distillation of Winston Churchill's life as a statesman, politician and national leader; and full of reminiscences of his and Lady Churchill's personal life at the house.

his private secretary, Sir John Colville, known as Jock, in 1962 that started the 'Jock' tradition at Chartwell. The first Jock was ginger, with white paws and chest, and was one of Churchill's favourites, even appearing with him for his grandson's wedding photographs. After Churchill died, his wife asked that there should always be a Jock kept 'in comfortable residence' at Chartwell, a wish still honoured by the National Trust, who acquired the house in 1966. Jock outlived Winston Churchill by nine years, and he is buried in the little pet cemetery in the gardens. Jock II lived with the head gardener, and was known for being extremely free with his paws, which must have caused those charged with keeping him 'in comfortable residence' to act with considerable restraint.

When Caroline Bonnett arrived at Chartwell with her partner Neil Walters to take up their respective posts as assistant visitor services manager and house manager, it was on the understanding that caring for Jock III went with the job, and Jock made it very easy for them. On going into their apartment for the first time, there was just one chair, on top of which, smiling at them and purring like a sewing machine, waited Jock III. He was loved by everyone at the house, and had the rather charming habit of sitting on a bookshelf next to a framed photo of himself. Caroline and Neil looked after Jock III for two years, during which time he was the subject of numerous press articles and media attention: he even caught the attention of a Japanese magazine, who came over

specifically to do a photo shoot of him, which was the only time anyone could recall Jock III being intentionally difficult. Everyone at Chartwell was very upset at his eventual demise.

After a few months of getting used to Jock III's absence, the mandatory quest for a new Jock got under way. The RSPCA and the Cats Protection League were briefed as to the necessary specifications – marmalade, the right size of white bootees, nose and chin, but it took a while. Then one of the volunteers, David Hatter, came across the perfect candidate. Caroline and Neil visited him: they checked out the specs, and then the announcement was made. Jock IV had been found!

When Jock IV came to Chartwell, there was a welcoming tea party in his honour, and he played his part, rolling over good-humouredly, gazing at everyone with his golden eyes, as if to say, 'If I was a really mean cat, there'd be nothing you could do about it.' But he's not a mean cat: he's rather affable, if a bit lazy. A year and a half after his arrival he still hasn't got the hang of his role as a crowd-puller – he prefers to catch forty winks in the wardrobe. But still he is loved and cared for – although perhaps not quite as spoilt as he would have been if Winston Churchill were still alive.

Miss Pushkin and
Dame Kyrie Pussy Willow
Craigievar Castle

'No man ever dared to manifest his boredom so insolently as does a Siamese tom-cat when he yawns in the face of his amorously importunate wife.'

Aldous Huxley

Daphne Rose is the custodian of Craigievar, and lives in a cottage close by with her two cats Miss Pushkin and Dame Kyrie Pussy Willow, whom I shall refer to as DKPW, partly for purposes of brevity, and partly because any creature less damelike would be difficult to imagine.

Daphne has had a lifelong passion for cats, starting on HMS *Bermuda*, on which she, her mother and her father – a lieutenant commander in the Royal Navy – sailed to South Africa. On board, Daphne met the admiral's cat, a lordly and most unlikely ship's cat, and confided in the admiral that she too would like to have such a cat. Shortly after their arrival in South Africa, the admiral's official Rolls-Royce pulled up at the

HISTORY

Craigievar is thought to be one of the best surviving examples of the Scottish tower house. One of two family homes, it was built in the early part of the 17th century. The presence of ornamental plasterwork on the ceilings is unusual, at a time when interior decoration of a tower house was more likely to be in the form of tempera painted scenes, and the castle retains some fine original Jacobean furniture. In the first half of the 19th century, the then owner Sir John Forbes commissioned the architect John Smith to re-roof Craigievar, and to implement a number of other major reforms and repairs. Curiously, Craigievar is a very early example of a historic house open to visitors. Queen Victoria visited more than once, on one occasion incognito.

house, with two Siamese kittens curled up on the back seat. Since then Daphne has never been without a cat.

When Daphne moved to Edinburgh she was accompanied by a Siamese called Ella Fitz, named more for her vocal nature than her ability to emulate her namesake's exquisite vocal abilities. Daphne eventually took a post with the National Trust of Scotland as custodian of Craigievar Castle. She was out in the garden picking gooseberries, when out of a nearby clump of fennel emerged a well-fed but disorientated tabby, obviously lost. Cats have an astonishing way of picking a home when one is needed: Ella Fitz gave a half-hearted hiss of discouragement at this latest arrival, who ignored her completely, strolled over the doorstep into the house, went upstairs, plonked herself on a spare bed and went to sleep. Attempts to find the owner failed, so Miss Pushkin came to stay.

After Ella Fitz's death, Daphne decided to maintain the tradition of her two favourite combinations of cat: tabby and oriental. She contacted a local Burmese breeder, and acquired DKPW. Miss Pushkin, in an ironic re-enactment of Ella Fitz's reaction to her arrival, hissed like a ruptured boiler and walked out in a fit of rage. It didn't last long: there was a small question of food, rain, and the icy winds that sometimes sweep the castle estate and woodlands. After a few days of lurking morosely near the cottage, she came back in. It wasn't long before both cats were engaged in a reasonably friendly tug-of-war at either end of a long piece of string. DKPW is a typically nosey Burmese, wanting to see everything, climb everywhere and get into everything, and she developed an animated relationship with Miss Pushkin. The kitchen, being constantly warmed by the stove, is the obvious place for both cats to tarry, but if Daphne thought that she might have peace and quiet, she was mistaken. Cupboard doors are hooked open, or suddenly open from within to reveal a cat blinking in the unaccustomed light; shelves are scrambled along; objects on said shelves are scattered like confetti; anything like a photo or notice pinned to the wall is immediately inspected, and usually pulled down; things are dragged from one end of the kitchen to the other; pot lids are removed; and, as for knitting, well – forget it. DKPW wasn't the only culprit. Miss Pushkin, though older, suddenly developed a most un-tabbylike sense of oriental curiosity, rushing at discarded newspapers and knocking things around in true Burmese style.

And if this energetic domestic behaviour wasn't enough, the castle and grounds really got the treatment! Although neither cat is allowed in the main part of Craigievar, both go to the reception area and office, where they 'assist' with the paperwork. Both walk with visitors to the castle from the car park too. Actually, neither cat *walks* anywhere: in the open air they dash in and out of bushes, leaping on to trees, waiting behind hedges, wriggling rear quarters in preparation for a surprise ambush. Outdoor play is relentless: how else can one explain a cat being startled by nothing? Miss Pushkin and DKPW *want* to be startled. Most of the bushwhacking is reserved for each other: they'll spill out of the cottage with Daphne when she goes for a walk; and from then on it's pouncing paradise. Progress round the castle grounds is a succession of leaps, surprise pounces on one another, feverish scrambling up tree trunks, where both cats often ending up staring wildly around on a branch not strong enough to support a mouse, let alone a cat. These cats have fun. Oh yes, there *are* visiting dogs sometimes, but they are strongly urged not to molest the custodian's cats.

Tosca and Aida
Drum Castle

'In a cat's eye, all things belong to cats.'
Old English saying

Alec Gordon is not a traditional cat person: after 27
years as a wing commander in the Royal Air Force, he
decided to start a second, less high altitude career in
the National Trust for Scotland, and, in the early years
of living at Drum, installed three amiable and very
well-fed black Labradors: Holly, Bracken and Rowan.
It was only after he had met his Japanese wife, Rika,
that cats came as well. Rika has a traditional love of,
and fascination for, cats, and no objections, even from
a retired wing commander, would stop her getting
them. Alec reluctantly accompanied Rika to see some
kittens at a nearby farm: the breeder had high social
aspirations for her kittens, and informed them that her
kittens could only go to someone who lived in a castle.
It was the quiet pleasure Alec took in retorting that

HISTORY
Drum Castle has stood watch over the River Dee since
the twelfth century, when the tower was given by
Robert the Bruce to William de Irwyn; his family, the
Irvines, continued to live at Drum for over six
centuries until 1975, when the castle passed from
Henry Quentin Forbes Irvine, the 24th laird, into the
care of the National Trust of Scotland. In the 17th
century the ninth laird built the Jacobean Mansion
that now abuts the tower house. This was a significant
break with tradition; for the first time an occupier of
Drum extended the ground area of the castle.
Previously, and reflecting troubled and uncertain
times, tower houses had been expanded at the top,
keeping their defensive characteristics, and giving rise
to the classic tower house shape – narrow at the base,
and broader at the top.

they did live in a castle that persuaded him to take not one but two kittens.

Alec called one Tosca, and Rika named the other Aida, after their favourite operas. The dogs and kittens took a little while to get used to one another, and for the first few weeks viewed each other through a screen: the cats with suspicion, the dogs with typical Labradorean friendliness. When the time came to make formal introductions, Alec took charge. Tosca and Aida were put in the living room, and each dog was consecutively marched in to receive a ceremonial swipe of warning. Poor dogs: the last one in had to go to the vet! However, the time had come to integrate the animals of the household. The cats would look on with envy as the dogs were taken out for walks and Aida, though the shyest of cats, even took to creeping down the spiral stone steps after them. This was not encouraged, as Aida shows some of the characteristics of her operatic namesake – namely a propensity for concealing herself in closed spaces – and, in a building full of motion sensors and alarms, this led to some panic-stricken dashes by the Gordons.

At first the two kittens gave the poor dogs a hard time, leaping at them, on to them, attacking tails and ears as if the cats' lives depended on it. After an exhausting few months of guerrilla activity, Aida and Tosca came to realise that these three jocular Labradors meant no harm, and scaled down hostilities. Aida and Rowan developed an inexplicably close relationship: they cuddle up together at every opportunity, but when anyone comes across this touching scene, both animals spring apart in acute embarrassment, as if caught in *flagrante delicto*. When Aida wasn't associating with Rowan, or sitting with Alec and Rika, she was busy learning to conceal herself from all visitors, even those whom she came to know. The head gardener Diane Robertson and her two daughters kindly look after the cats if the Gordons are away, and Aida even hides from them. She's not very good at it though: a large lump moving stealthily under the tablecloth is a dead giveaway.

Tosca, following Alec Gordon's previous career path, took to high altitude antics. He found a window at the top of the tower turret that gave him a spectacular view of the courtyard below, with all the coming and going of visitors. He stands on the tower window ledge, above a vertiginous drop to the castle courtyard. Tosca enjoys the startled reaction this elicits from visitors to the castle; his plaintive miaows are just a tease to induce panic in those who happen to spy him tottering on his lofty window ledge. Tosca and Aida live life from the inside: the spacious rambling rooms occupied by Alec and Rika offer ample opportunity for exercise and activity. Tosca is fascinated by the painter who works at the top of a long ladder, repainting the window frames; he stands on tiptoes, his paws scrabbling energetically at the window glass while the painter tries frantically not to lose his balance outside. Both cats love Christmas too – particularly the large

Christmas tree, which they scramble up, shedding glass balls, to emerge through the foliage at the top, like two furry angels. It's a position that is hard to hold for very long, as the combined weight of both cats sets the tree swaying alarmingly, sending Tosca and Aida tumbling to the floor, along with the tree. It gives a whole new meaning to the term 'fallen angels'.

Saddam and Gremlin
Erddig

'There is, incidentally, no way of talking about cats that enables one to come off as a sane person.'

Dan Greenberg

A sign on Glyn and Deborah Smith's courtyard cottage at Erddig proclaims 'Chats Lunatiques' (Mad Cats, for the non-French speaking reader). And inside, one of the first things that strikes the visitor is a series of photographs on the wall of Glyn sitting extremely close to a very large tiger, leading one to wonder whether it is 'les chats' of the household who are mad, or a certain head gardener.

Glyn Smith has been at Erddig for 21 years, overseeing a garden that was first landscaped in the 18th century. The walled garden is considered by many to be one of the most important in Britain, containing rare and historical examples of fruits. The Moss Walk now houses a National Collection of ivies, and elsewhere there is a

HISTORY

Erddig was built for Joshua Edisbury on his appointment as High Sheriff of Denbighshire in the late 17th century. It is impressive in scale, if plain. In the 18th century the house was purchased by John Meller, a successful London barrister, who furnished the house lavishly, and much of his furniture can still be seen at Erddig. Meller bequeathed Erddig to his nephew Simon Yorke, whose son Philip Yorke initiated extensive 'improvements' and renovations, not all of which were wholly sympathetic to the history and style of Erddig. By the 20th century, the house was in disrepair, structurally compromised by coal-mining. The third Philip Yorke, however, employed local people to help with running repairs, and obtained compensation from the coal board. The house was handed to the National Trust in 1973 and is now restored to its former glory.

canal, fishpond, and a restored Victorian yew walk. The herb border has many of the plants that were used in the day-to-day running of the house, and, opposite, the old Drying Green, once used for laundry bleaching and drying, now supports cob nuts and fruit trees.

There's an historical precedent for cats and gardeners at Erddig. Sharp-eyed visitors to the house might spot the cat curled up in the 19th-century portrait of Thomas Pritchard, the first Erddig gardener to be immortalised on canvas. The Smiths' first cat at Erddig was Nibbles, a healthy and well-fed tabby who was found wandering in the garden. No one could find out where Nibbles had come from – Glyn thinks she may have been a stowaway in a visitor's car – and she moved in with the Smiths. Deborah brought the next cat back from Wrexham. Glyn was emphatic that it had to go. So it clambered on to Glyn's lap, and thence on to his shoulders, and stayed. At first the recent arrival was a bit of a brute: he'd push Nibbles away from the food, and the children wanted to call him Rambo. But, as he took over more and more of the house and gardens, it was decided that Saddam might be a more descriptive name. Both Saddam and Nibbles were people cats, preening themselves in front of visitors, and generally putting in as many public appearances as possible. Saddam managed to wind his way around the feet of the Prince of Wales during the 25th anniversary of the opening of the house by the National Trust. After having the Royal calf rubbed by Saddam, the Prince wryly asked Glyn whether Saddam was a member of staff.

In the meantime, Deborah spotted another cat in need: this one was crossing the road in a very peculiar way, walking as though she had been at the whisky bottle. She thought that she may well have been abandoned, and rescued her on the spot. The family thought that she looked like a gremlin (the Steven Spielberg/Joe Dante variety), and so she was named. Gremlin is a real special needs cat, with a nervous system disorder that she lives with very cheerfully; as if sensing her frailty, Saddam and Nibbles simply let her into the family without fuss. Gremlin is cautious, and, although she seems to like visitors, contents herself with gazing at them from under the gate into Glyn and Deborah's cottage. Saddam loves visitors too; he takes an evening promenade to meet the public, and still follows Glyn around the gardens. I say still, for Saddam is both blind and deaf. How he finds his way around is a mystery, but he does, and even goes into the shire-horse stable to chew on the horse nuts. He must be using the senses of touch and smell, far more advanced in a cat than in a human. But the longevity and happiness of both Gremlin and Saddam is a tribute to a household of great kindness.

Oh yes, those tigers. Glyn has always been fascinated by big cats, and was given a contact session with a tiger cub as a Christmas present. Off Glyn went, eagerly expecting a cuddly little cub, only to find that his contact session was with a seven foot long tiger (ten if one counts the tail and whiskers)!

Mozart
Eyam Hall

'Dogs come when they're called. Cats take a message and get back to you.'
Mary Bly

Robert Wright, a direct descendant of Eyam Hall's original builder Thomas Wright, inherited the Hall 17 years ago, and, until recently, he and his wife Nicola lived there with their children Jeremy, Felicity and Timothy. Jeremy is now taking over the running and administration of the Hall, and, in doing so, is inheriting a cat called Mozart.

Mozart is by no means the first cat to live at Eyam Hall. When the house was first opened to the public, a rescue cat called Tigger took up residence. He was, by all accounts, a bit of an exhibitionist, and would lead guided tours around the house, stopping impatiently to look over his shoulder if he thought that the groups were taking too long. When the time came to find a

HISTORY

Eyam Hall, a rugged Jacobean family house in the 'plague' village of the same name, is situated in Derbyshire's Peak District. It is still occupied by the descendants of Thomas Wright. The Hall was built of local gritstone; it is a no-nonsense family home with low mullioned windows, built to withstand the winter winds and snows that blast down from the moors. The Hall is most emphatically a family place, with a pleasant and welcoming collection of historical furnishings, paintings and fabrics. In the nursery can be seen toys belonging to previous generations of Wrights, mixed up with a model railway layout belonging to one of the Wrights' sons – as elsewhere a reassuringly un-museumlike blend of the historic and the personal.

new cat, the same cat rescue organisation that had placed Tigger put Robert in contact with someone who was nursing a litter of kittens. There were some constraints about choice, however: Nicola was adamant that they should not have a white cat; Felicity expressed a dislike of ginger cats; as Robert is the person in the house who most likes cats, he felt that really he should have the last say. The choice was wide – tabbies of all sorts of stripes and patterns, or plain black – and so, perhaps as a subtle reproach for all this feminine colour bias, he carefully chose a kitten whose colour would be calculated to offend the colour sensibilities of both his wife and daughter. He came back triumphantly to the hall with a ginger *and* white kitten. It was a fait accompli of course: no one was going to reject this appealing little colour faux pas of a kitten.

After the usual few days of settling in, without a name yet, the kitten started to explore the Hall. He liked the Victorian nursery, and made his bed in an old doll's pram; he also came across a rather fine grand piano and a harpsichord, both regularly played by the family. Although a leap on to the piano keyboard gave him the fright of his life, he became fascinated by both piano and harpsichord, and his regular strolls along the keyboards of both gave rise to his name – Mozart. Mozart made his own 'music', sometimes at unsociable hours, giving rise to rumours of ghostly activities, which rivalled the alleged phantom of a drowned servant girl. He also acquired an acute interest in the mechanics of the pianoforte, forever trying to catch the hammers as they rose to strike the strings. Mozart liked the harpsichord too, but found the stiffer action of the keys more difficult to manage.

Like his illustrious namesake, Mozart is temperamental: there's always activity in and around the Hall, some of which he clearly dislikes. The Motley Mutt dog show is one event that he avoids like the proverbial plague, while the annual Easter egg hunt is more congenial. Then there's Lulu, a West Highland terrier belonging to Nicola: definitely not one of Mozart's favourites. When Lulu's about, Mozart isn't! He either retreats to the top of the nearest cupboard, or heads for the hills. In fact he does a lot of retreating: faced with a camera, and having pleaded for about half an hour to be let out, he wedged himself firmly under a sideboard. There is a wilder side to Mozart too: he often goes out on the razzle, arriving back at the Hall in the early hours looking distinctly the worse for wear.

With such a glorious home in which to live, one might expect Mozart to have adopted any cosy area of the house, but he prefers the boiler room, through the wall of which has been constructed a 'cat tunnel', permitting Mozart a quick escape route to the great outdoors, should anything offend or irritate him.

Sybil and Bodmin
Feeringbury Manor

'Even overweight cats instinctively know the cardinal rule: when fat, arrange yourself in slim poses.'
John Weitz

Most abandoned or lost cats are picked up in considerable distress, being subsequently homed through one of many worthy animal rescue centres. Bodmin, one of two cats at Feeringbury Manor, had a different approach. He's a 'self rescue' cat.

It happened thus: one cold winter's evening the Coode-Adams family was enjoying a peaceful and informal meal in the warmth of the large manor house kitchen. The weather outside was mournful and rain rattled against the windows. As Sonia Coode-Adams left the table to secure the cat flap, which the wind had started to rattle violently, the head of a very wet and determined-looking cat thrust through the opening, glaring around like a cantankerous, animated

HISTORY

Feeringbury Manor is a pretty 14th-century lath and plaster building, surrounded by an established garden and adjacent to the river Blackwater. Its original hall was split into two storeys in the 17th century: the manor is the family home of the Coode-Adamses, and contains many interesting features, including traces of late medieval stained glass. Henry VIII granted the manor to the Bishopric of Westminster in 1540, and, under Edward VI, Feeringbury was passed to the Bishops of London. The house is not open to the public, but visitors are welcome to the extensive and intensively planted gardens, which include a working Victorian watermill, and a series of striking galvanized steel sculptures by artist Ben Coode-Adams.

gargoyle. The family watched in astonishment as this bedraggled, purposeful marauder dragged himself through the cat flap: he stood dripping rainwater onto the flagstone floor and looked around, daring anyone to try to put him out. Then he headed straight for the cat food, which he polished off without pausing for breath: the family was impressed and decided, without truly having much choice in the matter, that they would let him stay.

Other animal occupants of the household were not so untroubled. Arthur, a tabby and white tom-cat, was chased around by the new arrival, who had now acquired the name of Bodmin after the mysterious big cat that roams the gloomy rainswept Bodmin moors at night. Poor old Arthur never recovered from the shock

of this invasion: he took up quarters in a woodshed for five years, receiving spiritual counselling during the regular visits by one of Giles Coode-Adams' relatives who was a nun.

There was another cat observing this mayhem too: Sybil is a 'Grande Dame' Persian, a mixture in personality of Oscar Wilde's Lady Bracknell and Muriel Spark's Miss Brodie – a cat that was accustomed to having things very much her own way. She was no waif and stray: Sybil had been purchased from a very upper crust pet store in London's Pimlico, and spends most of her time looking disapprovingly at everything. Sybil even eats Persian food: melon, avocado and cooked French beans are at the top of her food preferences. She considers Sonia to be her personal servant, and Sonia describes her as being 'grumpy and picky', then goes on to add affectionately, 'I suppose really she's vain and stand-offish.' It goes without saying that Sybil regarded Bodmin as oafish and coarse, but what would Bodmin make of her? Well, oddly, he never bothered her, he seemed to hold her in awe, and did his very best, without any success, to flatter her at any opportunity.

There were some accommodations to be made: the manor house, a delightful if modest 14th-century building, is not open to the public. But the ten or so acres of garden in which it is set are, and reflect Sonia's touch as a former garden designer, and husband Giles's influence – he's a council member of the Royal

Horticultural Society; the gardens are varied, and include a small arboretum of trees grown from Kew Gardens seed-collecting expeditions. Sybil frequently and disdainfully dismissed Bodmin from the house, and it was lucky for Bodmin that the head gardener Ellen Fairbanks likes cats, and made sure that Arthur was secure in his woodshed when the ravening black beast was out and about. Actually this is all a bit unfair: Bodmin has a very sunny side too, although those who make the beds in the house would tell you otherwise. Bodmin lurks under beds. The safest way to take off bedcovers and sheets is quietly to take hold of one corner, and then suddenly run for the corner of the bedroom, dragging the bedding behind you at high speed. This way Bodmin only gets to sink his claws into the bedlinen, rather than your hands. It really makes one wonder why on earth he was adopted in the first place!

When it comes to the other animal in the house, springer spaniel Millie calls the shots; Bodmin and Sybil become reluctant participants in an endless game of chase. Sybil gets out of the way by going high, while Bodmin dashes through the flowerbeds to the arboretum, where he sharpens his claws on highly prized specimen trees in readiness for a return to the fray.

OPENING PAGE AND LEFT
Bodmin makes himself at home
RIGHT
Sybil looks on disdainfully

Sasha
Finlaystone House

'Never wear anything that panics the cat.'
P J O'Rourke

Sasha, a mild-mannered tabby-and-white cat, lives with Kate Pinkerton, her two children Penny and Nicky, and partner Donald, in a cottage on Finlaystone Estate. Kate runs the Celtic Tree cafeteria, catering for visitors to the gardens and estate woodlands. The estate is a haven for wildlife of all sorts and sizes, some prized for their rarity, and some – namely rodents of every description that had moved into the cottage that the family were taking over – not so welcome. The rodents completely ignored the family dog, Ceilidh, who didn't even notice them, so Kate decided that a cat should be an essential part of the household. She'd had cats before: two chinchillas, and an affable ginger fellow called Ben. Sasha was found abandoned, and her new home on Finlaystone estate was like a dream come true.

HISTORY

The present house at Finlaystone is built on the site of an original 14th-century fortified building, and has been a family home for over 600 years. It is in an extensive estate with spectacular views across the Firth of Clyde. Finlaystone is currently home to the Chief of the Clan MacMillan, George Gordon MacMillan, and his family. It was extensively rebuilt in 1760, when the old castle bailey was demolished and replaced by a new house. A Glasgow architect, John James Burnet (who designed the King Edward VII Gallery in the British Museum), introduced further changes in 1900, and it is the Burnet interiors for which the house is now known, together with the gardens and estate.

George MacMillan and his family, in conjunction with the estate rangers, take a keen and active interest in the horticulture and educational aspects of the garden and estate, and part of Finlaystone is a designated Site of Importance for Nature Conservation. The gardens and woods – an interesting combination of lawns, scented gardens, wild woodland walks, burns and waterfalls – are all open to the public. They contain an exceptional range of wildlife, from bats and otters to one of the largest heronries in southwest Scotland.

So, with an absence of traffic, a cottage with tall pine trees nearby to clamber up and woodlands and gardens to explore, it is an ideal home for a foundling cat. Sasha loves high places and running water, and spends hours on end watching waterfalls: her favourite viewpoints are from a variety of trees. She completely ignores Ceilidh, who quivers with unrequited longing

to play games with her. Oddly, and thankfully, Sasha shows no interest in the wide variety of birds that frequent the woodlands: this may have to do with an unexpected and very unsettling encounter with a heron shortly after her arrival at Finlaystone. She is similarly wary of the recently arrived ducks and chickens, all of which are larger than she, and far more assertive.

A lot of the estate visitors come to walk their dogs and often they stop at the café for a drink and something to eat. Sasha likes going down to the café with Kate, or to see her there, and her favourite pastime, apart from checking out the menu of the day, is dog teasing. Her arrival is normally marked by an outbreak of hysterical barking from visitors' dogs, whose leashes are attached to the table legs. The extendable leads are the most interesting, and Sasha often sits up a tree, watching, with quiet satisfaction, the canine chaos that sometimes follows her arrival, as an ever-expanding tangle of leads winds round chairs, tables, people, and other dogs. No dog has yet pulled free to pursue Sasha, but her appearance at the Celtic Tree usually results in radical rearrangements of the outside table layout, and a lot of spilt tea. Sasha has an ulterior motive for coming down to the restaurant: Kate now does the catering for the MacMillan family's shooting parties and, though Finlaystone House is uncompromisingly 'doggy' and the house is a flurry of canine activity, the MacMillans usually remember to send a goodly portion of roast venison up to the restaurant for Sasha.

Mole, Titch and Casper
Great Dixter

'The clever cat eats cheese and breathes down rat holes with baited breath.'
W C Fields

Christopher Lloyd didn't like cats; his favourite animal companions were rather irritable dachshunds. But his trusted gardeners did, and still do. Foremost among the cat champions at the house are Fergus Garrett, the head gardener, and Perry Rodriguez, the business manager.

Fergus's first cat came via his partner, Amanda, who had a cat called Roger – a slightly odd name for a cat, I felt – that she had found dodging the swirl of traffic on London's Holloway Road. Aha, Roger the Dodger of course! Roger moved with Fergus and Amanda to Hastings, eventually dying at the good age of 18. By this time, the cat bug had bitten Fergus: a Roger II was a priority, and came in the form of Simsek (Turkish

HISTORY

The earliest part of the house to survive the passage of time is the Great Hall, built in the mid-15th century for Richard Wakehurst. In 1910 the house passed into the ownership of the Lloyd family, and it was Nathaniel Lloyd, together with the then young architect Edwin Lutyens, who gave Great Dixter its present form. Their method was unusual: it involved dismantling an early 16th century house in a nearby village, and incorporating it into the manor house at Dixter. The gardens, for which Great Dixter is rightly celebrated, are the work of Christopher Lloyd and his parents, largely based on a design by Lutyens. The house is surrounded by garden: meadow to the front and side; yew topiary; the Sunk and Barn Gardens; and bold and adventurous mixed borders. It's fascinating and highly individual, a joy to both horticulturalist and novice.

for lightning). Simsek was chosen on the grounds that he was the only kitten in the litter to bite Fergus: assertiveness was an essential quality for any cat having to cope with Christopher Lloyd's dachshunds. More replacements for Roger came via a friend of the family who needed to find a home for three cats, Mickey, Mole and Titch. A speeding car cut Mickey's life short, but Mole and Titch hung on, and came with Fergus, Amanda and Simsek to Great Dixter. There was a lot of snorting about cats when they arrived, both from Christopher Lloyd and the dachshunds, but, in the iconoclastic spirit that constantly inspired the gardens, the cats were tolerated.

Both Mole and Titch have made their homes in the gardens: the nursery sheds were adopted as a base, where they can often be seen snoozing among bags of compost, plants for sale, garden tools and general bric-a-brac, waiting for the weather to improve so that they can set out on their garden rounds. Simsek, in contrast, has a more domestic nature. Despite having been chosen for his feisty spirit, he has shown the least inclination to confront the dachshunds, and spends most of his time as a pillow for Fergus and Amanda's daughter Ayse.

Titch and Mole's new accommodation brought them into contact with Casper, Perry Rodriguez's stocky and companionable black-and-white cat. Casper is very visitor friendly, but is quite a tough fellow too. He is partial to a pizza every now and then and he's the cat that brought the dachshunds to heel; local rabbits have also found out that being in the gardens doesn't enhance prospects of longevity when Casper is around.

Titch and Mole have become a little more distant with each other; the trouble centres on a wall along which both cats like to walk, starting simultaneously at opposite ends. They both stroll towards each other in an unconcerned manner until they get close, when the carefree stroll gradually transforms into a wary sideways hunch. At this point both cats studiously avoid looking at each other and neither wants to give way. Hackles rise and tension builds at the mid-wall stand-off: sometimes there's a quick bout of slapping; at other times one or other grudgingly yields right of way, jumping down with an irritated hiss.

So Titch and Mole tend to lead separate lives. Titch is always on day and night patrol around the gardens and house, while Mole has made friends with Casper: they chase each other around the nursery, and, when the garden is in the grip of a hard winter night's frost, Mole and Casper, rather than staying curled up in the warmth, dash and skid around on the icy paths like a pair of uncoordinated four-footed skaters.

OPENING PAGE
Titch on patrol
LEFT
Mole on the disputed wall
RIGHT
Casper, who tamed the dachshunds

Lucy
Hardwick Hall

'Most cats when they are Out want to be In,
and vice versa, and often simultaneously.'
Dr Louis J Camuti

Lucy is a Manx cat, one of that curious breed
originating on the Isle of Man, and was acquired by
Nigel Wright when he was assistant keeper of the
social history gallery of the Manx Museum, a bastion
of 'Manxism' on the Isle of Man. When Nigel and his
wife Lindsay first came back from the Isle of Man to
live in Chorley, where Nigel was curator of Astley
House, they brought with them Lucy, and another
Manx cat, Possum. They – the cats – never got on that
well: whenever Lucy passed Possum, she'd bat her
round the head, and that seemed to be the extent of
the relationship! Possum succumbed to an early
kidney infection – a common cause of illness among
Manx cats – and Lucy came with the family to
Hardwick Hall, where Nigel and Lindsay live with

HISTORY
Hardwick Hall is one of the grandest Elizabethan
houses in Britain. It was built in the 16th century for
Elizabeth, Countess of Shrewsbury (more commonly
known as Bess of Hardwick); the architect was Robert
Smythson, who also built Longleat for Sir John
Thynne. The hall is most noted for its large multi-
paned windows, and the carved 'ES' crests that top
each of the six towers projecting from the house.
Inside, the house is much as it was during Bess's time,
with original plasterwork, fireplaces, carved furniture
and 16th-century tapestries. The house is in the
ownership of the National Trust.

their daughter Breesha in an apartment in the old service quarters of the Hall. This sometimes foreboding, but ever intriguing, house built of dark sandstone looms over the surrounding countryside, its carved open balustrades and ornate crests proclaiming to all and sundry the power, wealth and position of its original owner. Hardwick Hall has its own stonemasons, who are engaged in a rolling programme of repair and restoration of the house; consequently, there is often scaffolding on one or more parts of the house exterior. This offers Lucy a fairly safe way to explore the house, and a good lookout point from which she can see whether or not Mickey, one of the estate warden's cats, is waiting for her. Lucy's early days at Hardwick were not without incident; Mickey had previously chased both Lucy and an unfortunate passing squirrel up a tree. (Despite the lack of tail, Manxes have good balance, and like to climb.) Both cat and squirrel sat on a branch waiting for Mickey to lose interest, which took some time. Since then Lucy has always been sympathetically disposed towards squirrels.

This breed of cat has some odd characteristics, the best known of which are a stump for a tail, and rather spindly rabbitlike rear quarters. One of the curiosities of Manx cats is that, within the same litter, one can find kittens with differing lengths of tail, and the island has a different island name for each type of tail length: Rumpy, (Rumpy-)Riser, Stumpy, and Longy (all sound to me like a collection of dwarfs from a Disney cartoon, rather than styles of cat). A Rumpy has no tail at all; a (Rumpy-)Riser has a small stump; a Stumpy has a short stump of a tail; and a Longy a clearly visible, but still short, tail.

So which is Lucy? I had a good look and there is certainly a stump there. But what defines the transition between a small stump and a short stump? I couldn't tell, so decided to create a new category for Lucy: Lucy is either a Stumper or a Rimpy! But, whatever she is, she certainly has some of the behaviour characteristics of a Manx cat: she is very vocal, for a start. There's no need of a cat flap; when Lucy wants to come in she warbles at the office door or bedroom window.

What Lucy likes most is to get inside things: boxes mostly, though her preferred enclosed space is Breesha's doll's house. This has led to a slightly stormy relationship with Breesha, who says that she loves Lucy except when she's in the doll's house. Since the doll's house is not much larger than Lucy, one can understand Breesha's frustration as the cat scatters furniture, dolls and dolls' clothing left, right and centre in her struggle to insert herself into the first floor section. It is also very odd to stand by the doll's house, and suddenly become aware of a large eye watching one from out of a miniature window.

Now that she is established, Lucy clambers on top of fences to watch visitors arrive; and if Nigel is out and about in the main part of the house, he doesn't have to worry about Lucy being locked out in the Derbyshire rain. Lucy makes sure that *someone* hears her calling to be let in, and then it's simply a matter of calling him up on his radio. Given the size of Hardwick Hall, he gets good exercise and, if he's too far away, he can always claim that reception wasn't very good that day.

Orlando
Hellens

'Cat angels are the reason there are no mice angels.'

Mel Brooks

Orlando is the large affable marmalade cat at Hellens; he belongs to Ottilia, the daughter of Nicholas Stephens, sculptor and curator, and his artist wife, Carmel. Ottilia chose Orlando for her ninth birthday; she selected him from a litter on a nearby farm because he was pot-bellied, bandy-legged and had an air of constant surprise. His colour was also a perfect match for the rich red brick of Hellens.

There were already two resident animals in the house – a diminutive and highly strung terrier, Milou, and Torta, a brindle cat whom Ottilia had found in a hedge in a Herefordshire village. Torta lives upstairs now, in the Stephens' family apartment: she's old and not too well, although Ottilia thinks of her as very original and

HISTORY

Hellens Manor in Herefordshire is a rambling Jacobean manor house hidden at the end of a long track leading from the nearby village of Much Marcle. This is an enchanted house whose oak-panelled rooms are rich with period furnishings, paintings and decorations. Four-poster beds abound, and there are heirlooms of Ann Boleyn, Mary Tudor, the Earl of Essex, Charles I, the Duke of Wharton, and others of the house's inhabitants over the centuries.

The gardens have been redeveloped along Tudor and Jacobean lines, and include a 17th-century octagonal dovecote, a yew labyrinth, a walled knot garden, and a short woodland and pond walk. A 16th-century tithe barn and hay wain barn have been restored, and are used for community and cultural events.

Although run by a trust, Hellens is first and foremost a family home: every room has a story to tell, and the house is littered with family memorabilia and reminders of the frequent presence of the family at the house. The family hosts music recitals, poetry, drama, art and garden events throughout the year, and, from an early age, Orlando determined that he would play a part in as many of these events as he could. But, before he could really join in, Orlando had first to learn to negotiate the spiral stone staircase that curls steeply down from the Stephens' apartment. Each stone step was about twice his height. Once the staircase was mastered, his first attempts to become involved in house parties met with mixed success. Eating all the butter in the kitchen while supper was being prepared for twenty or more people was not a big hit, and neither was his interest in chess, which culminated in a valuable ivory chess set being reduced to rubble. Standing his ground against the family dogs was met with more admiration: it's quite something to see a half-husky, half-wolf scrambling to get away from a bristling ball of hissing ginger-and-white fur.

highly eccentric; her eyes have changed colour several times, each eye independent of the other! Torta didn't much mind another cat, whereas Milou had a fit of furious jealousy, retreating under the dining table from whence came a constant stream of canine invective. Orlando blithely ignored this unwelcoming reception. He was going to enjoy life in this rambling and decidedly unconventional country home.

Orlando learnt to try not to upset anyone: he behaved as a good cat should, curled up in front of a blazing log fire, keeping quiet while musicians were performing, and generally, if reluctantly, giving up his fireside seat should a guest want to sit there instead. He also learnt that one certain way of getting attention is to join the groups that go around the house, and is often seen twining himself around the legs of visitors while they listen to explanations and descriptions of the priceless art and furnishings that pack every corner of Hellens. He also sometimes sleeps in some of the most haunted parts of the house and reports no unusual activity, which is more than can be said of some of his human counterparts. When Orlando sleeps, it takes more than a spectre to wake him up.

Outside, the gardens offer equal delight for this roly-poly marmalade cat: walled gardens; a maze; woodland walks and ponds are his pleasant outdoor territory. And in these gardens a mélange of ducks, chickens and rabbits waddle and hop around, largely ignored by Orlando, who, in his youth, had a painful but educational encounter with an extremely protective and indignant mother duck. He does love trees though: a person wandering through the garden might suddenly have a feeling of being watched and, looking around, might spot Orlando stretched out along a branch, gazing down at them with curious blue-green eyes. Outdoor events are a regular feature of life at Hellens, and Orlando recently disgraced himself at one. Ottilia's school staged A Midsummer Night's Dream: the whole performance was interrupted by Orlando hopping on and off the stage, very much in the spirit of the capricious mischief afoot that night, but with a devastating effect on the young actors' abilities to remember their lines.

In the winter, when the house is closed to the public and winds howl round the barley twist chimney stacks,

Orlando avoids the chillier parts of the house, preferring to toast himself in front of a log fire, then burrowing into bed with whichever family member is too fast asleep to nudge him off.

Alcibiades
Kentwell Hall

'When a Cat adopts you there is nothing to
be done about it except put up with it until
the wind changes.'

T S Eliot

As well as being a Tudor house of considerable
historical interest, Kentwell Hall is the home of a
ginger-and-white cat called Alcibiades. It might be best
to untangle the names at this point: Alcibiades is the
name the cat was given by Patrick Phillips, the owner
of Kentwell Hall. Why a garden cat should be named
after an Athenian known as much for his capacity for
treachery as his political and military abilities, I don't
know, and the name has proved a mouthful for others
at Kentwell: the gardeners, with whom Alcibiades
spends much of his time, call him either Charlie or
Henry; visitors simply call him Puss. He doesn't seem
to mind, and either responds to all of them, or ignores
them all, as takes his fancy.

HISTORY
John Clopton, a wealthy local landowner, built
Kentwell Hall in the early 16th century. From the
outside the Hall retains its original appearance,
surrounded by one of the largest moats in the country.
Adjacent to the main house is a rare 15th century
service building, containing a bakery, dairy, brewery
and solar, all still being used for their original
purposes. The present owners, Patrick and Judith
Phillips, have worked continuously on restoring the
house, gardens and outbuildings, whose interior
features several fine Tudor rooms, including the
working Great Kitchen and Great Hall with its
Minstrels' Gallery. The grounds include a home farm,
a 17th century style walled garden that retains its
original basic layout, whilst in the courtyard there is a
Tudor rose maze.

Alcibiades first appeared in the gardens, where he was adopted by the gardeners. Patrick Phillips, by his own admission, is not a 'cat person', but, for some reason, he took to this rugged marmalade cat. Patrick Philips avers that Alcibiades talks to him with clear 'miaows' of meaning, and likes the fact that the cat knows what he wants, can convey it easily, and is tidy and clean. In a traditional farming environment, all have to earn their keep, and while Albiciades may not be able to best the rats, the local mice have hastily moved out. The rare breeds farm is an intrinsic part of Kentwell Hall life: one of the first animals, a Jersey cow, provided the

family with milk, and now Tamworth pigs, Longhorn cattle, Suffolk Punch horses and Poitou Donkeys are all successfully bred and kept, with a clucking clutter of poultry and fowl that scuttle through the farmyard and grounds. Most of the animals are in keeping with Kentwell's Tudor character, and figure in painstakingly detailed Tudor life recreations pioneered by the Phillips. There are farm cats too: shy and furtive creatures that are fed in the farmyard, keeping very much to themselves.

Alcibiades is the cat with a public profile, and the only one who ever enters the main house. And that was as a result of a ferocious encounter with an unknown aggressor, leading to a short period of hospitalization. He was taken into the house to convalesce, and not surprisingly Albcibiades took a liking to life in the Hall; it was after this that he showed his communicative nature. He's not a shy cat either, and visitors often come across Alcibiades sitting on the parapet of the moat bridge, intently watching the koi carp churning the waters below: if he's in the mood, he'll take a companiable walk with visitors, often leading them on a garden tour, although as a garden guide Alcibiades can be a bit unpredictable, as he has the habit of suddenly disappearing and reappearing again. He's also a frequent participant in the Tudor life recreations that are held at Kentwell. The aroma of spitted meat wafting from the Tudor kitchen in the 15th century service buildings is irresistible, and he's not averse to a drop or two of small ale.

As the house remains a family home, independent of external grants and funding, income needs to be generated, to which filming, special events, corporate functions and weddings all contribute. Generally Alicibiades makes himself scarce when there are big events, especially noisy ones, with the exception of some of the outdoor concerts: he hangs around backstage for opera, both light and classical. When it comes to Elvis Presley Tribute nights, and the sousaphone, bagpipes and trombones of the nine piece funky folk band Bellowhead, Alcibaides heads for the old potting sheds on the other side of the Hall, where he lies, paws over ears, until silence falls. Alcibiades spends most of his nights either in the

warmth of the potting sheds, or flitting from shadow to shadow in pursuit of any mouse foolish enough to appear in the walled garden, thus possibly adding to the reassuring number of ghost tales which abound about Kentwell; those of a nervous disposition who join the Halloween Ghost Tours have been known to take quite a fright at Alcibiades's sudden rustling in the undergrowth.

Baby Puss and Tiger Moth
Nether Winchendon House

'We brought with us in the ship a cat, a most amicable cat and greatly loved by us; but he grew to great bulk through the eating of fish.'
St Brendan

Nether Winchendon is a house where cats and dogs tumble over one another in a jumble of cheerful domestic chaos: 15-year-old son Edmund, an excellent cook, busies himself in the kitchen, while daughter Isabel, a teacher, tries to organise her mother Georgianna. In the midst of all this, Robert Spencer Bernard works on his legal briefs, accompanied by an animal entourage comprising a lurcher called Sonic, and Shimmer the whippet, and, until recently, also a cat called Kip.

Unusually for a country house where traditional English country sports are enjoyed, cats enjoy equal status with dogs at Nether Winchendon. Kip was one of Robert's favourites: like all the family cats, he had

HISTORY

Nether Winchendon House is a wonderful example of architectural and historical whimsy. Though its origins are medieval – the Great Hall is believed to date back to the twelfth century and the reign of King John – the bulk of the house is Tudor; with a frivolous and charming overlay of late eighteenth-century gothic battlements and arcades. This is the home of the Spencer Bernards, whose forbears have been in occupation for the past 400 years: there are family portraits dating back to the 17th century, and innumerable examples of fine English furniture. The house, a family home in every sense, is open to the public. It is also used as a film location, and a restored barn offers an unusual venue for weddings and other events.

OPENING PAGE
Baby Puss on the balcony
LEFT AND RIGHT
Tiger Moth practising take-off and landing

come from the Blue Cross, following the family tradition of second-hand rescue cats. Kip showed a doglike devotion to Robert, forever talking to him, always walking to heel around the house, and, when the prospect of a walk was in the offing, Kip would streak through the cat flap like a charging bullock.

Two more cats came to live at the house – Tiger Moth, a stripy, part leopard–spotted, and very definitely sporty, cat, and Baby Puss, a Blue Burmese crossed with something else. Kip tolerated these two new arrivals with resigned good humour: what else could such a gentlemanly fellow do with two kittens that relentlessly pounced on one's gently twitching tail? With Kip's passing, Tiger Moth and Baby Puss were left to establish their own particular territories. Sonic and Shimmer had to be taught that the two young cats were not squirrels to be chased up trees. This was quickly achieved by the application of sharp claws. Baby Puss became the house cat, living upstairs. She does come down, mostly to lead visitors around the house, but, as dusk falls, she is normally to be found roaming the rooftops, watching the bats wheel around the Tudor chimneys and through the archways.

Tiger Moth is more of an outdoor sort of chap: not intentionally named after the legendary flying machine, he nevertheless displays the same capacity for altitude and aerobatics. He dashes across the lawns towards the River Thame, launching a mad scramble up the nearest tree, and completely overlooking the

choice of laps on which to sit. Of course there are the weddings too and, with bridal couples encouraged to do their own thing, these present a bizarre range of attractions, from sit-down Bangers and Mash dinners to fibreglass cattle in the nearby fields. These last had Tiger Moth completely confused, as the cattle he knows tend to get restless when he's around. Cooking is a major attraction for both cats, uniting them in unusual common purpose. Edmund's culinary magic in the kitchen always attracts the cats, and a recent television production of *Stately Suppers* in the house had Baby Puss and Tiger Moth drooling: the tantalising aroma of crayfish and honey-roast duck drew them inexorably from upstairs and the garden.

Filming is something that the cats enjoy taking part in: location caterers are always good for a soft touch, although endless bacon sandwiches can get a bit tedious. Baby Puss is fascinated by life on the set: the house has been used as a location for BBC productions of whodunits such as the *Midsomer Murders*, Agatha Christie mysteries, as well as a James Bond adventure, *Tomorrow Never Dies*. Many a director has torn his hair out when, in the midst of the denouement, Baby Puss either streaks through the shot, or walks calmly up to the principal actors, bumping against their legs in friendly greeting.

fact that it is always far easier to go up than to come down. And, if living in such wonderful surroundings was not sufficient, the cats have an impressive range of events and activities to draw their attention. Tiger Moth often sits on one of the two bridges that span the river, wishing he could whisk trout out of the water with the ease of the local fly-fishermen. He likes the orienteering too, and dashes along with the participants, trying to explain that he knows a far better short cut. Baby Puss likes to join the more cerebral events: spiritual healing, painting, sculpture and craft activities are more her style as these offer a

LEFT
Tiger Moth pleading to be let out
RIGHT
Baby Puss cornered on the balcony

Fluffy and Ariel
Sezincote

'To bathe a cat requires brute force, perseverance, courage of conviction… and a cat. The last ingredient is the hardest to come by.'

Stephen Baker

Sezincote has a formidable feline pedigree. Edward Peake's grandparents Sir Cyril and Lady Kleinwort purchased the house in 1944, bringing with them the Siamese cats for which she had a passion. In fact, both grandparents were so well disposed towards cats that the grandchildren referred to them as Grancat and Grantom, and it was quite common to see Lady Kleinwort striding around the estate in deep conversation with one or more attentive Siamese cats at her side. The last pair of Siamese cats to live at Sezincote with her were Anna and Akbar. At Sezincote the phrase 'walking the dog' was completely turned about: no one walked a dog at Sezincote; they all walked the cats. Edward's mother walked cats, as did Edward, who had broken with tradition by acquiring

HISTORY

Sezincote is one the Cotswolds' most surprising and unusual houses. This extraordinary Georgian Mughal confection is set in magnificent English landscaped grounds and is home to Edward Peake, his wife Camilla and two young children. The estate was purchased in 1795 by Colonel John Cockerell on his return from Bengal. He commissioned his brother Samuel Pepys Cockerell to design, with the landscape artist Thomas Daniell, a house that would combine elements of Hindu and Muslim design, exemplifying the principles of religious tolerance promoted by Akbar the Great, ruler of the Mughal Empire in the 16th century. The interior of Sezincote, however, was initially decorated in the style of Greek Classical revival; it was only in the early 19th century that Charles Cockerell modified it to an 'Indian' style.

two Burmilla cats, Ishtar and Asherah. They frequently kept Edward company as he walked round the lake, dashing madly across the grass one minute, strolling nonchalantly at his heels the next.

In due course Ishtar had kittens; actually she was always having kittens. Like the Siamese before her, she also had a vigorous love life. The family seemed to spend more time on homing the kittens of these wonderful and promiscuous cats than on anything else: all the cats on the estate have something of the original lineage. One of Ishtar's progeny was homed in the nearby town of Broadway: she eventually had kittens, one of which – Fluffy – was brought back to Sezincote by Edward. Fluffy is black and long-haired, a sociable and easy-going chap. He likes young people, and particularly looks forward to visits from Oscar, Edward's ten-year-old son. He patiently indulges two-year-old Lochie, one of whose games is to get Fluffy's tail tickling his face. The cat obliges, and the house echoes with shrieks of delight as Fluffy patiently whisks the tip of his tail back and forth across Lochie's nose.

Yet another descendant, a granddaughter, of Ishtar – Ariel – came to live at Sezincote. A diminutive wide-eyed tabby, she is so named for her fascination for playing with the aerial on a small television set in the house, an amusing trick until one actually wants to watch a programme (television picture quality on an indoor antenna in the Cotswolds is primitive at the best of times). Ariel didn't have much 'street' sense: if being kicked by a horse wasn't bad enough, she then got in the way of a reversing Land Rover. Ariel did recover from her injuries, but, from that point on, has

OPENING PAGE AND LEFT
Fluffy has the run of the house
RIGHT
Ariel prefers the warmth of the nursery

taken life a lot easier. In the winter she can usually be found sleeping in a cosy basket in the children's upstairs nursery rooms, where it is customary to pay her a visit; one always gets a very cordial welcome and it's a little like going to see one's convalescing grandmother. In the summer, Ariel picks her way carefully down the main staircase to join the family, taking the sun on the terrace outside the orangery, and joining in the guided tours of the house.

There is a little animal tension in the household. Camilla's lurcher Frankie is constantly chided by the cats while inside the house – 'No you can't lie there; get away from my food bowl; you're hogging the fire' sort of thing – and Frankie frankly gets a bit fed up. So he gets his own back by making sure that Fluffy gets plenty of tree-climbing experience in the gardens. Both Fluffy and Ariel are part of the guided tours in the house; they lead visitors into the bedrooms and hop up on to the beds as if to say, 'Now, this is very comfortable. We suggest you all sit down with us, and we'll just have a short nap on your laps.'

LEFT
Fluffy watching her visitors
RIGHT
Ariel in her bed

Bandini, Sidney and Eliza
Southside House

'A cat is more intelligent than people believe, and can be taught any crime.'

Mark Twain Notebook, 1895

Visitors to Southside House should be aware that they are likely to be waylaid by the two newest feline residents, Bandini and Sidney. These two portly and good-humoured brothers coexist in more or less peaceful circumstances at the house, and are among the most jovial of all the country house cats, making themselves known to visitors by leaping out of the hedges miaowing plaintively (and rather feebly for their size) in an attempt to convince anyone naïve enough to pay any attention, that they are underfed and ignored; they are clearly neither malnourished nor neglected, but it doesn't stop them trying to elicit totally unwarranted sympathy.

Bandini, Sidney and Eliza, the present trio of resident

HISTORY

With 17th-century origins, this eccentric and slightly dilapidated house is a refreshing antidote to many of its formal and grander counterparts. Its mostly William and Mary-style architecture and interiors have been subject to imaginative and romantic restoration and reconstruction. A maze of passages, galleries and rooms, packed with treasures and art, lead the visitor through a journey of family histories, with reminiscences of Royal visits, literary figures, family scoundrels and the lives and loves of those who have lived here, while the faint aroma of wood smoke and the burnt candle stubs in holders around the house are reminders that the past maintains a distinctive hold on Southside House and those who live there now.

Robert around the house. The arrival of Bandini and Sidney changed everything for Eliza: she'd tolerated the enthusiastic attention of adminstrator Richard Kendall's dog, an affable, curious, but rather uncertain, dalmatian, but the arrival of two large cats was too much. After delivering a few telling blows, Eliza decided to live aloof from the antics of these two happy-go-lucky newcomers, and she now haunts the nearby King's College School (where Robert and Ruth strongly suspects that she supplements her diet). And while Bandini and Sidney now astutely avoid any confrontation with Eliza, they have assumed the role of house clowns. Bandini has made his home with Tim Vize-Martin, the head gardener, and Sidney unpacked his case on a shelf above the Aga in the Munroes' apartment. They are both thespians at heart, an appropriate attribute for animals in a house that epitomises melodrama and theatricality.

Animals are an intrinsic part of the recent history of Southside: owls, dogs, cats and horses have all lived here, and the house and gardens are still a refuge for foxes, birds, squirrels and wildfowl. The sense of the place of animals in the life of the house is touchingly illustrated in the charming but rather odd ivy-festooned pets' cemetery, a jumble of homemade memorials and carved effigies in an overgrown corner of the garden. Animals abounded here: the three Munthe children, who lived in the upstairs nursery, had cats and dogs; their father Malcolm Munthe had a horse, his pet owl Romolo, and a variety of dogs; and

cats, were introduced by Ruth Munroe, a professional singer and vet's daughter, and her husband Robert, deputy cultural administrator of the house. Eliza, the first of the three to arrive, is a small, one-eyed foundling with a bullish attitude towards other cats. As the only cat in the house, she'd turn up for guided tours, wait for visitors at the main gate, and accompany

the charm of it is that this brouhaha of animals still exists. Sidney and Bandini fit happily into this mêlée, barging their way into the introductory talks given to visitors, wandering along with guided tours, and supplementing discourses on art, history and family life with sotto voce miaows.

In the gardens, things are a little different. Bandini shows less than fraternal affection for Sidney, and skulks in the undergrowth waiting to leap out on his unsuspecting brother, and poor Bluebell the Dalmatian doesn't fare much better. She's always inexplicably delighted to find Bandini in a shrubbery, unwisely poking her nose through the foliage to say hello – a greeting that is invariably returned in the form of a hefty biff.

Although historically interesting in its own right, with origins in the mid-17th century, the Southside House that visitors see today has been largely shaped by the endeavours of one particular person, Malcolm Munthe, son of heiress Hilda Pennington and the famous Swedish doctor and author, Axel Munthe. In the 1940s the house was in poor condition, having been left more or less unoccupied during the Second World War. Malcolm Munthe set about recreating a home to match his idealised and romantic view of the past. Trompe l'oeil ceilings, flamboyant fireplace mouldings, a whole host of domestic treasures and family memorabilia emerged to jostle with the extraordinary wealth of art and furnishing that

OPENING PAGE
Bandini on the south terrace
LEFT
Eliza prefers street life
RIGHT
Bandini on a garden expedition

characterise this historic house, while, in the gardens, classical temples and grottoes sprang up in unlikely corners. Southside is clearly and delightfully still a family home, and its animals are an intrinsic part of life in the house.

Away from the public gaze, Sidney spends his life roasting gently on the shelf above the Munroes' Aga, while Bandini drives Tim mad by constantly wanting to either come into or out of their first floor rooms: he is the 'devil cat', Tim mutters in exasperation, as he endlessly goes up and down to open the garden door for Bandini. He's thinking of devising a basket on a rope and pulley in which he can lower and lift the 'devil cat', but, given the contrary nature of cats, and Bluebell the dalmatian's affable curiosity, he's more likely to find Bluebell, rather than Bandini, dangling outside his window.

LEFT
Bandini in reflective mood
RIGHT
Sidney keeping an eye out for Bandini

Frisbee,
Mr Mephistopheles
and Mr Norris
Tissington Hall

'The cat is domestic only as far as it suits its own ends.'

Saki

Frisbee, Mr Norris and Mr Mephistopheles have been at the Hall for several years, and, in their various ways, have almost become part of the background scenery. This ability that all three cats have of melting into the background was inspired by the arrival of Tuskar, a Rhodesian ridgeback. Mr Mephistopheles, an eighth birthday present for daughter Francesca, melted so far into the background that he quit the Hall entirely, taking up residence in the old vicarage grounds, where he now lives in dog-free peace in a greenhouse. He still comes over the wall into the Hall, skulking in a plantation of small Christmas trees waiting for Francesca as she leads her pony through the stable yard. Truth to tell, Francesca is the only person he seems keen on: anyone else coming across Mr

HISTORY

Francis FitzHerbert built Tissington Hall on the southern slopes of Derbyshire's White Peak District in 1609, replacing an older, moated manor. It is set in the centre of the village of the same name, in an extensive estate populated largely by tenant farmers. The FitzHerbert family have lived in this fine Jacobean mansion without interruption for nearly 400 years. The architect Joseph Pickford improved the Hall towards the end of the 18th century. At the beginning of the 20th century a wing was added, housing the library and billiard room. Tissington is an idyllic English country village, complete with duck pond, cottages and a delightful Norman church. The Hall is a home to Sir Richard FitzHerbert, ninth baronet, his wife, Lady Caroline, and their children Francesca and Freddie, and has only recently been opened to the public.

in the north wing. He likes the peace and quiet, the attention, and the access to the roof, from where he peers down through the parapets. It's where he can usually be seen at dusk: like a feline gargoyle, he sits motionless beside Oscar the owl (one of the most prominent of a set of carved animals that crown the parapets). Frisbee's nights are spent sleeping all over the house. He favours the library and the west drawing room, mainly for the soft furnishings, but he'll settle anywhere where there's a warm hearth.

The conversion of the old stable block into a kindergarten and pre-prep school was cause for rejoicing among all the cats. Encouraged to come into the classrooms by gleeful youngsters, the cats were quick to appreciate the finer points of education in the early years; Mr Norris and Frisbee enjoyed the kindergarten home corner, where they were honoured guests. And, after being offered incessant cups of tea, plates of imaginary biscuits and cakes, the two cats would curl up contentedly on the carpet to listen to a story. Frisbee also found his way into the gymnasium, where he'd nonchalantly demonstrate to the younger children the finer points of vaulting, jumping and climbing. Mr Mephistopheles was a little more disruptive: his thing was art, and many a painting left out to dry has been augmented by a random pattern of paw prints. Mr Mephistopheles was suspended from the school when he began to show an unhealthy interest in the sandpit.

Mephistopheles among the Christmas trees is likely to be fixed with a demonic glare worthy of his devilish namesake.

Mr Norris and Frisbee are a little more resilient, and held their nerve when Tuskar took up residence: it's amazing how smallish cats can persuade a large dog that playing boisterously, eating the cat food, barking loudly and generally being over lively is simply not a good idea. The cats' domestic tranquillity is also helped by a kindly lady called Carol, who has set up an impregnable roost for Mr Norris and Frisbee in the laundry room. It's warm, and conveniently near the scullery.

Mr Norris has struck up a friendship with Lady Caroline FitzHerbert's mother, Mrs Shooter, who lives

The cats habitually wander with visitors through the village to the duck pond, taking care to give a wide berth to irate mother ducks. They also come out for one of Tissington's most celebrated occasions, the Annual Well Dressing Festival: they really enjoy the confection of coffee beans, flower petals, moss, bits of pasta and so on that are used to illustrate a bible scene or well-known hymn title. They are nevertheless discouraged from using the well dressings as multi-coloured scratching panels, or from climbing on them; Frisbee created quite a stir when he peered out from around the top of one notable well dressing depicting the 'mysterious stranger'. There is much else in the general life of the village to interest the cats: a tearoom; a plant centre in the old kitchen gardens; and a recently opened butchery, outside which the cats sit longingly, noses twitching in unrequited appreciation.

Acknowledgements

Arley Hall – Emily Jane Foster;
www.arleyhallandgardens.com

Bateman's – Rooney Elaine Francis, and the National
Trust; www.nationaltrust.org.uk

Brodsworth Hall – Chester and Bertie Michael
Constantine, Dan Booth, and English Heritage;
www.english-heritage.org.uk

Cairness House – Missy a.k.a. Newton Julio Soriano and
Khalil Khairallah; www.cairnesshouse.com

Capesthorne Hall – Marmalade Stephen Caldwell;
www.capesthorne.com

Chartwell – Jock IV Caroline Bonnett, and the National
Trust; www.nationaltrust.org.uk

Craigevar Castle – Pushkin and Dame Kyrie Pussy Willow
Daphne Rose, and the National Trust for Scotland;
www.nts.org.uk

Drum Castle – Tosca and Aida Alec and Rika Gordon,
and the National Trust for Scotland; www.nts.org.uk

Erddig – Saddam and Gremlin Glyn and Deborah
Smith, and the National Trust; www.nationaltrust.org.uk

Eyam Hall – Mozart Robert and Nicola Wright;
www.eyamhall.com

Feeringbury Manor – Sybil and Bodmin Sonia
Coode-Adams; www.ngs.org.uk

Finlaystone House – Sasha Kate Pinkerton;
www.finlaystonehouse.com

Great Dixter – Mole, Titch and Caspar Fergus Garrett
and Perry Rodriguez; www.greatdixter.co.uk

Hardwick Hall – Lucy Nigel and Lyndsay Wright, and
the National Trust; www.nationaltrust.org.uk

Hellens – Orlando Ottilia Stephens;
www.hellensmanor.com

Kentwell Hall – Alcibiades Patrick and Judith Phillips,
www.kentwell.co.uk

Nether Winchendon House – Baby Puss and Tiger Moth
Robert and Georgianna Spencer Bernard;
www.netherwinchendonhouse.com

Sezincote – Fluffy and Ariel Edward and Camilla Peake;
www.sezincote.co.uk

Southside House – Bandini, Sidney and Eliza
Tim Vize-Martin and Robert and Ruth Munroe;
www.southsidehouse.com

Tissington Hall – Frisbee, Mr Mephistopheles and Mr
Norris Sir Richard FitzHerbert; www.tissington-hall.com